Vaclav Nelhybel

Duets

for horn and trombone

e.c. kerby ltd.

DISTRIBUTED BY

HAL•LEONARD®
CORPORATION

7777 W. BLUEMOUND RD. P.O. BOX 13819 MILWAUKEE, WI 53213

DUETS

for Horn and Trombone

VACLAV NELHYBEL

Vivo (♪ = 200 ca.)

Horn

1.

Trombone

Tumultuoso (♩ = 100 ca.)

2.

3.

Allegro marcato (♩=160 ca.)

4

Vivace (♩ = 168 ca.)

4.

Vivo (♩=160 ca.)

5.